Kumaian
MIRROR OF DESTINY

Kumalak
MIRROR OF DESTINY

Ancient shamanic wisdom from Kazakhstan to reflect your past, present and future

ADAPTED BY
Didier Blau

BOOK PUBLISHING

NOTE TO THE READER
Before you consult *Kumalak*, please check the number of beans included in your pack. More than 41 beans may have been inserted during the packing process, and therefore if you find any extra beans we suggest that you put them to one side and keep them as spares.

A CONNECTIONS EDITION

This edition published in Great Britain in 1999 by
Connections Book Publishing Limited
St Chad's House, 148 King's Cross Road
London WC1X 9DH

Text copyright © Didier Blau 1999
Illustrations copyright © Dave Hopkins/Ian Fleming Associates 1999
This edition copyright © Eddison Sadd Editions 1999

The right of Didier Blau to be identified as the author of this work has been asserted by him in accordance with the British Copyright, Designs and Patents Act 1988.

All rights reserved. No part of this publication may be reproduced, stored in a retrieval system, or transmitted in any form or by any means without the prior written permission of the publisher, nor be otherwise circulated in any form of binding or cover other than that in which it is published and without a similar condition being imposed on the subsequent purchaser.

British Cataloguing-in-Publication data available on request

ISBN 1-85906-031-5

First Edition
1 3 5 7 9 10 8 6 4 2

Phototypeset in Goudy and CgSkjald using QuarkXPress on Apple Macintosh
Origination by Bright Arts PTE Ltd, Singapore
Printed and bound in China through Leo Marketing, UK

Contents

Prologue 6

About Kumalak 10

Understanding Kumalak 14

Consulting Kumalak 16

Combinations 20

THE READINGS

The First Row 24

The Second Row 41

The Third Row 58

Reading Special Figures 75

SAMPLE READINGS 80

The Long-term Future 86

Record Sheets 92

Acknowledgements 96

Prologue

A map of the world is pinned on the wall. Yellow, ochre, red … the steppe of Central Asia spreads out like a palette right to the edges of the Orient. Images of the past, of all times, mingle, crowd my mind: caravans heavy with silk and spices crossing the deserts, magnificent cities buried in ancient sands, floods of Genghis Khan's barbaric hordes, tales of Joseph Kessel and his horsemen bathed in sunlight … One more time, they inspire me to make a journey.

As my destination, I choose Kazakhstan, a new country recently created out of the ashes of the Soviet empire. On a chilly yet sunny morning in September 1994 the jet lands at Almaty – formerly known as Alma-Ata – after having flown over yellow, ochre and red

Map showing Kazakhstan and surrounding area

LEFT *In the central market of Almaty, the locals seek guidance from the Kumalak soothsayer.*

OVERLEAF *Earth, sand, water and open space are the elements to be found along the 'Silk Trail', birthplace of Kumalak.*

vastness, the very same colours that transfixed me on the map. Nevertheless, reality doesn't live up to my dreams. For seventy years, the Soviets' presence in Almaty transformed the city into a waste of concrete cubes and asphalt, a dormitory town. Endless queues at shop doors, old ladies hunched on the pavement selling ragged dolls and worn lace, trams unhooked from their disconnected rails ... to be sure, the wind of the steppe doesn't blow here.

I discover Kumalak at the open market. Caught between a currency trader and a peasant selling her bread, the old woman manipulates broad beans, sorts them and lays them out mysteriously on a piece of cardboard. 'An old Kazakh trick,' my interpreter, Jenis, tells me with a disdainful pout on his face before adding, 'a fortune teller.' Raised under Communism, he dismisses the ancient Kazakh's customs in general and anything irrational in particular. Neither the old woman nor Jenis are willing to tell me more about it – the former for fear of unveiling a secret that provides her with a living, the latter for fear of being seen as a believer and traditionalist at a time when Kazakhstan is being reborn and is opening itself to modernity.

Why didn't this story end there? Ignorant of the Russian language, not to mention Kazakh, I was at the mercy of Jenis – a student obviously more interested in rock 'n' roll, blue jeans and Coca Cola than in old tales. But fate – if it really exists – decided otherwise. At the French embassy, nestling at the heart of this strange and melancholic city, I met Aigul, the press attaché. At first surprised by my quest for information, this young Kazakh lady confessed, with obvious embarrassment, her interest in Kumalak. She explained the basic rules, then introduced me to her friend Gulia, a French teacher, expert in Kumalak.

After a phone call, she welcomed me to her tiny apartment located in the depths of a housing project. Facing the red ball of the Asian sun which bathed the fabrics and the polished wood table, she talked at length of this divinatory art, which has come from ages past and deep in the steppe, where her ancestors lived freely among sheep and horses. Her grandmother and then her mother taught her how to play Kumalak, how to make these forty-one broad beans speak. Today, she can afford to be outspoken. The Soviet system has perished, the ban on fortune telling is no longer enforced and Islam is not yet strong enough to re-establish the edicts of Communism.

We met for the first time in this sunbathed room, savouring meat balls accompanied by vodka. The broad beans were no longer mere broad beans, but messengers bearing news, advice and wisdom. Kumalak's spell was gradually taking me over, and in the depths of my soul I could feel its evocative power still intact after lying dormant for so long. Man's joys, sorrows and hopes have not changed, for ever blind to time and space. I received this initiation as if I had always known about it, the same way people did in the golden age of Samarkand or in the days of caravaneers, soothsayers and geomancers who travelled the Silk Trail. Aigul Kuspanova, Gulia Sadikova and Cécile, my wife, travelling companion and muse, fill my thoughts today as I present the reader with this divinatory art discovered in a tiny living room of a building in Almaty.

About Kumalak

An ocean of land burned by the sun, frozen by the winter, swept by the wind, the Kazakhstan steppe spreads out under the boundless sky. Next to a yurt, the nomad's felt tent, a man has come to seek advice from the shaman. He is sitting next to him, his face solemn, his eyes staring at the soothsayer's fingers. Around them, a crowd drinks khoumys, the fermented mare's milk that warms the heart. The crowd gets closer, tightens … and grows silent. The shaman opens the Kumalak oracle. He lets a few dozen broad beans slip from his hands. Slowly, conscientiously, he separates them, sorts them and lays them on the ground, following a mysterious order. He then names the figures and interprets the signs: 'Earth in the head, water in the eyes … you are not free, your soul is darkened.' He continues, 'Horseman of fire on horse of wind … fear not, a star shines on your forehead, everything will be all right.'

The soothsayer announces the oracle with a slow and solemn voice. He proceeds as in times past, when caravans filled with fabrics and spices joined the Orient to the Occident. It is here, on the Silk Trail, that astrologers and geomancers coming from India, Arabia, China and Europe met and unveiled some of their knowledge. It is here that Bhal, 'the mirror of destiny', was born – the former name of Kumalak whose origin is lost in the mists of time. According to legend, the prophets Daoud (David), Danyar (Daniel) and Jacub (Jacob), as well as Korkyt Baba (Zarathustra) were the first keepers of these secrets. The Kumalak oracle, a divinatory art thousands of years old, came close to disappearing in the seventeenth century under the growing pressure of Islam, and then more recently under the Soviets who banned its practice. Today, it has reappeared publicly at the open market of Almaty, Kazakhstan's largest city, witness to a culture that is allowed to express itself anew.

About Kumalak

The Bhalcha

In the steppe, the man capable of predicting the future is the shaman, or Bhalcha as the Kazakhs call him. Singer, poet, musician, soothsayer, priest and doctor, he is the guardian of religious traditions and legends. Using his kobyz, or violin, he rids the body and the spirit of the demons that inhabit them. The sounds coming from his instrument are the sounds of nature: the wolf's wailing, the bird's chirping as well as the human soul's moaning. The Bhalcha has great knowledge of nature, animals and man. He is the only one capable of establishing a link between the sky, the earth and hell, the three regions of the universe which are linked by an opening. It is through this very 'hole' that the gods descend to earth and the dead to the underworld. It is also through this that the Bhalcha's soul, in a trance, can soar to heaven and plunge to hell. He then interprets the signs he received there. It is because of this opening in the universe that Kumalak may not be consulted after sunset – for fear of the dead learning the fate of the living and influencing it.

This early-twentieth-century photograph shows a shaman, or Bhalcha, with his magical instrument – the 'kobyz'.

About Kumalak

The Mystical Numbers

Numbers are of great importance in the Kazakh tradition, and some of them are considered to have mystical powers. The numbers listed on these pages are all of special significance in Kumalak. For example, one, two, three and four correspond to the number of beans that are placed in each square during a consultation, and each has its own particular associations which are reflected in the reading. Seven, nine and twelve are important in relation to the 'special' fortuitous readings, while the forty-one beans used in Kumalak represent the Kazakh year and the beginning of a new period.

~ ONE ~

The number one is associated with fire. It represents flashes of lightning, the spark that lights the fire, crashing thunderbolts, the evening star that shines in the firmament. It symbolizes action, clarity and combat.

~ TWO ~

This number is associated with water: water that flows from the river, water that falls from the sky, as well as water in a pool that freezes to become a mirror. The number two symbolizes both the right and the left, good and evil. Number two has a double face, representing tension and imbalance.

~ THREE ~

The number three is associated with the air. It represents the wind, the breeze or thunder. It symbolizes the three realms of nature – animal, vegetal and mineral – as well as the three regions of Kazakhstan: the forest and lakes of the north, the great steppe of the interior and the sandy deserts of the south. It also evokes the three Kazakh nomadic populations: to the east, the 'great horde' of the masses; in the centre, the 'middle horde' of the wise men; and to the west the 'small horde' of warriors. Thus, the number three expresses journeys, encounters and the joining of forces.

~ FOUR ~

This number is associated with the four cardinal points whose centre is the great mountain Ouly-Taou. Earth is its element, earth from the steppe that provides grass for the sheep who, in turn, provide men with their basic necessities: meat, milk and wool. Thus, the number four symbolizes material wealth and possessions. But earth is also used to cover the dead, and sand is sometimes whipped into a storm. The number four is then associated with sorrow and darkness.

~ SEVEN ~

In Kazakh cosmology, the central pillar supporting the world comprises seven steps made of different metals in accordance with the seven planets. The first step is made of lead (associated with Saturn), the second of tin (Venus), the third bronze (Jupiter), the fourth iron (Mercury), the fifth 'monetary alloy' (Mars), the sixth silver (the Moon) and the seventh gold – the gold of Tengri, god of the sun and space.

~ NINE ~

According to Kazakh tradition, the Bhalcha must cross nine celestial regions before reaching the gods. The purpose of his journey is so that the Bhalcha becomes imbued with divine influences which he subsequently communicates to the humans. The Kumalak grid is also made of nine squares.

~ TWELVE ~

Product of the four cardinal points through the world's three planes, the number twelve is associated with time and space. It expresses totality, achievement and perfection.

~ FORTY-ONE ~

Forty-one is a sacred number. If one divides 360 days of the year by the magical number nine, it equals forty – the forty weeks of the Kazakh year. A proverb says: 'If you have already endured the year's forty periods, you can survive another period.' The remaining five days comprise this forty-first period that ushers in a new cycle.

Understanding Kumalak

Kumalak is a method of divination based on the interpretation of small objects (broad beans, coffee beans or other beans, for example) which are drawn from a bag and placed on a grid. In Kazakh, 'Kumalak' means sheep's droppings, the original item used. The shaman would dry them in the sun before laying them on a grid traced directly on the ground, and in this way would predict the future. A Kumalak grid is made of nine squares and each square is numbered, starting from the top right corner and working across the rows from right to left (*see above*). During the drawing, one, two, three or four beans are placed in each square.

The Kumalak Grid

The Kumalak grid represents a traditional Kazakh horseman of the steppes, with each square corresponding to a part of the body (*see below*). The combination of the relevant part of the body with the natural element represented by the number of beans, forms the traditional name given to each reading (for example, 'Fire in the head, sand in the eyes' and 'Water in the heart, wind in the hands'). By tradition, the name is formed from the central and right-hand squares in each row of the grid.

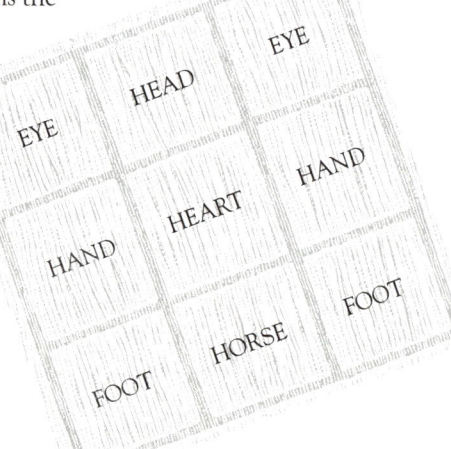

The Rows

The Kumalak grid is made up of three rows. Each row represents a different aspect of the reading, and is associated with keywords that reflect the way in which the reading should be interpreted.

THE FIRST ROW
The first row describes the past and its influence on the present. It represents the state of mind of the subject. This row evokes the clarity of his or her ideas, the tenor of their project, and thus their chances of being successful.
Keywords ~ The subject's spirit, thoughts and hopes. The path they are taking, what they believe in, how they foresee their predicament in the long term.

THE SECOND ROW
The second row describes the subject's present situation. It indicates the events they are currently experiencing, their deep feelings as well as their strengths and weaknesses. It also evokes the state of their health and their possessions.
Keywords ~ Heart, intuition, deep feelings, impressions, fears, doubts, power struggles and the subject's relationship with others.

THE THIRD ROW
The third row concerns the future. It represents the development of the situation, the answer to the question, the omen of the future. This row indicates what the subject can expect in the near future.
Keywords ~ Obstacles to overcome, action to take, journeys to make, behaviour to adopt.

Consulting Kumalak

To consult Kumalak you need to be in a calm, accessible frame of mind. In essence, you are 'laying yourself bare' before nature and the gods, and therefore you should not smoke or drink alcohol while consulting Kumalak, and also remove any jewellery or metal objects that may be on your clothing.

You can consult Kumalak both for yourself and for others. If you are doing a reading for someone else, the person must sit next to you, on your right (according to Islamic tradition, this is the 'good', safe side).

Asking a Question

You can ask a specific question on any subject – for example, to do with a relationship, a professional project, a journey, a friendship, a birth or your health. You can say the question aloud, write it down, or just say it to yourself, keeping it secret. But you don't have to ask a question – if you prefer you can simply consult Kumalak to see what advice it has to offer. In these instances your intuition – your gift for interpreting the future – will be at work. And with time and practice you will become a Shakerjan, a competent soothsayer, capable of not only foreseeing the future accurately, but also of giving helpful advice to those around you.

How to Make a Reading

In order to make a reading, you need to use the casting cloth and the 41 beans provided. You will be placing either one, two, three or four beans in each of the nine squares on the grid, and this will direct you to your readings in the book. Follow the simple steps outlined below to find out what to do.

1 Sit down at a table and lay out the cloth in front of you, with the grid at the top. Gather the beans together in a pile on the cloth, in the space underneath the grid. If you wish to ask a specific question, focus on it now before moving on to the next step.

Consulting Kamalak

2 Randomly divide the pile of beans into three smaller piles (don't count out the beans – the piles can be different sizes). Lay the first pile on the right, the second pile in the centre and the last pile on the left.

3 Beginning with the first pile (the one on the right), take away four beans at a time, until only one, two, three or four beans are left. Place these remaining beans in square number 1 on the grid, in the top right corner. Repeat this process with the middle pile, removing four beans at a time and placing the remaining one, two, three or four beans in square number 2 on the grid (top centre). And do the same with the third pile (the pile on the left), placing the remaining beans in square number 3 on the grid (top left corner).

4 Now gather together the leftover beans and once again divide them into three piles. Repeat step 3, but this time place the beans in squares 4, 5 and 6 (remember – begin with the right-hand pile).

Consulting Kamalak

5 Collect all the leftover beans together for a final time, dividing them into three piles. Again, repeat step 3, but this time place the beans in squares 7, 8 and 9 on the grid. You have now completed your grid, and can discard all the remaining beans. You will not need them again for this reading.

6 To check you have completed the procedure correctly you need to make a few quick calculations. If any of the lines do not add up to the numbers given below, go back to step 1 and start again.

a) FIRST ROW Add up the number of beans in squares 1, 2 and 3. The sum total should be either 5 or 9 (in our example it's 9).

b) SECOND ROW Add up the number of beans in squares 4, 5 and 6. The sum total should be either 4, 8 or 12 (in our example it's 8).

c) THIRD ROW Add up the number of beans in squares 7, 8 and 9. The sum total should be either 4, 8 or 12 (in our example it's 4).

Consulting Kumalak

Reading Kumalak

Your grid is now complete and you are ready to read it. Get a pencil and a piece of paper (or use one of the blank record sheets included at the back of the book) and draw your grid. Then check the tables of combinations on pages 20 to 22 and make a note of the figure numbers that correspond to the rows in your grid. When you have done this, go to page 23 and check whether any of the special figures are also applicable. If so, make a note of these too. The figures that relate to our sample grid are shown below.

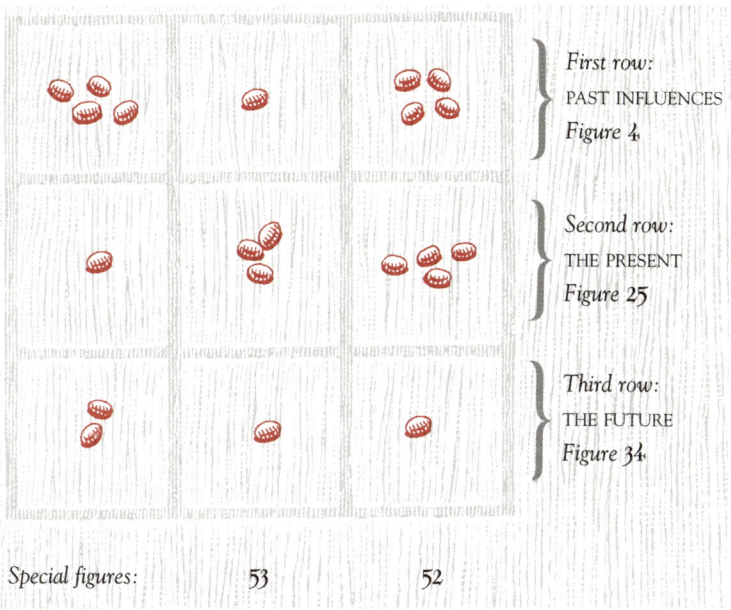

First row:
PAST INFLUENCES
Figure 4

Second row:
THE PRESENT
Figure 25

Third row:
THE FUTURE
Figure 34

Special figures: 53 52

To find out what Kumalak has to tell you, turn to the relevant readings in the book. So for this example you would read figure 4 to discover your past influences, figure 25 for your present, figure 34 for your future, and figures 52 and 53 as special readings.

Now that you know how to open Kumalak, you are ready to discover its ancient wisdom for yourself …

Combinations

First Row

 1 Fire in the head, wind in the eyes

 9 Wind in the head, fire in the eyes

 2 Fire in the head, water in the eyes

 10 Wind in the head, sand in the eyes

 3 Fire in the head, fire in the eyes

 11 The three stars

 4 Fire in the head, sand in the eyes

 12 Wind in the head, water in the eyes

 5 Water in the head, water in the eyes

 13 Sand in the head, sand in the eyes

 6 Water in the head, fire in the eyes

 14 Sand in the head, wind in the eyes

 7 Water in the head, sand in the eyes

 15 Sand in the head, water in the eyes

 8 Water in the head, wind in the eyes

 16 Sand in the head, fire in the eyes

Second Row

17 *Fire in the heart, water in the hands*

18 *Fire in the heart, fire in the hands*

19 *Fire in the heart, earth in the hands*

20 *Fire in the heart, wind in the hands*

21 *Water in the heart, fire in the hands*

22 *Water in the heart, earth in the hands*

23 *Water in the heart, wind in the hands*

24 *Water in the heart, water in the hands*

25 *Wind in the heart, earth in the hands*

26 *Wind in the heart, wind in the hands*

27 *Wind in the heart, water in the hands*

28 *Wind in the heart, fire in the hands*

29 *Sand in the heart, wind in the hands*

30 *Sand in the heart, water in the hands*

31 *Sand in the heart, fire in the hands*

32 *Sand in the heart, earth in the hands*

Third Row

$\overline{33}$ Horseman of water on horse of fire

$\overline{34}$ Horseman of fire on horse of fire

$\overline{35}$ Horseman of earth on horse of fire

$\overline{36}$ Horseman of wind on horse of fire

$\overline{37}$ Horseman of fire on horse of water

$\overline{38}$ Horseman of earth on horse of water

$\overline{39}$ Horseman of wind on horse of water

$\overline{40}$ Horseman of water on horse of water

$\overline{41}$ Horseman of earth on horse of wind

$\overline{42}$ Horseman of wind on horse of wind

$\overline{43}$ Horseman of water on horse of wind

$\overline{44}$ Horseman of fire on horse of wind

$\overline{45}$ Horseman of wind on horse of earth

$\overline{46}$ Horseman of water on horse of earth

$\overline{47}$ Horseman of fire on horse of earth

$\overline{48}$ Mother earth

Special figures

RIGHT-HAND COLUMN

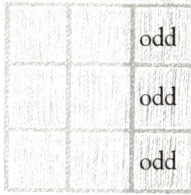 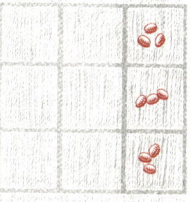 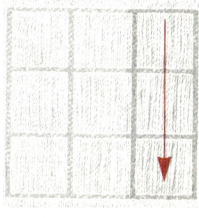

49 ◆ *Satisfaction*   50 ◆ *Inspiration*   51 ◆ *Good fortune*   52 ◆ *Chance*
Total = 7, 9 or 12

MIDDLE COLUMN

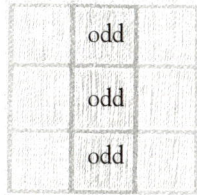 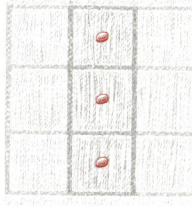 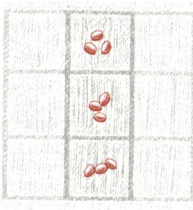

53 ◆ *Harmony*   54 ◆ *The way forward*   55 ◆ *Joy*

DIAGONALS

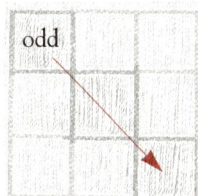  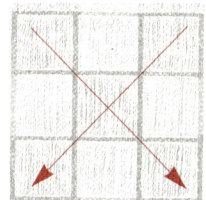

56 ◆ *News*
Odd numbers
in either diagonal

57 ◆ *Balance*
Sums equal in
both diagonals

THE READINGS

The First Row

THE PAST

Spirit

◆

Thoughts

◆

Hopes

◆

Beliefs

◆

Path

◆

Foresight

Fire in the head, wind in the eyes

YOUR STATE OF MIND
This is a very positive figure. You are clear-thinking, generous and receptive to the world. You are also very driven and are confident that your ideas will succeed. Your assets are your flexibility, your enthusiasm and your initiative.

IF YOUR QUESTION IS ABOUT …
A specific project ~ You have a high chance of success. The path you are following is in tune with your deepest aspirations, and you are at one with yourself, with no fear of problems or adversity.

A journey ~ You will find satisfaction and will return richer, whether in material or spiritual terms.

2. Fire in the head, water in the eyes

YOUR STATE OF MIND
Your need to share, to form healthy relationships, and to fight for a common cause characterizes your personality. Love, tenderness and sweetness come first for you. You seek domestic happiness, harmony in your love life and, on a professional level, team work.

IF YOUR QUESTION IS ABOUT ...
A specific project ~ Your wish to create or preserve a balance, to become the centre of a relationship or to gather people around you will be granted. You can expect some very good news.

Children ~ You will become fulfilled.

A journey ~ You will draw much gratification from it and will come back richer, materially or spiritually.

The First Row

Fire in the head, fire in the eyes

YOUR STATE OF MIND

Your mind is attuned to the positive, vastness, heights. Your self-confidence allows you to open doors, develop situations, motivate others. You fear neither competition nor problems.

IF YOUR QUESTION IS ABOUT …

A specific project ~ Your chances of success are great. You are blessed with dynamism and the necessary drive to realize your plans.

A journey ~ You will derive much gratification from a journey, and you will return richer, whether in material or spiritual terms.

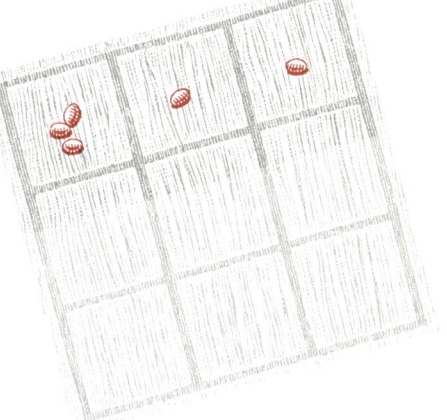

The First Row

4

Fire in the head, sand in the eyes

YOUR STATE OF MIND

You are worried, confused or disappointed. You are angry at someone or even at yourself, and you have doubts about the value of your project and the significance of your goal. Nonetheless, your thoughts are clear and you know what you want. If a particular responsibility weighs heavily at the moment, if the situation is slightly confusing, be certain that it will turn out positively, because your spirit is well focused.

IF YOUR QUESTION IS ABOUT ...

A specific project ~ Your chances of success are good, for your distrustful or sorrowful feelings will pass. You have all the qualities needed to bring about a positive result. Don't let your motivation abandon you because there is light at the end of the tunnel.

A journey ~ You will draw much satisfaction from it and will return richer, financially or spiritually.

Water in the head, water in the eyes

YOUR STATE OF MIND

Something irritates you or someone has offended you. Things are not developing the way you would like them to, or perhaps you feel like your fate depends on somebody or on your predicament. You lack the self-confidence that would give you strength to face other people. You don't have the tools to resolve your problems at the moment.

IF YOUR QUESTION IS ABOUT ...

A specific project ~ Your chances of success are slim at present, for you suffer from an inferiority complex or you feel powerless in the face of the current situation. To make a new beginning, you need to set aside an idea, a desire, some aspects of this project, or to give without expecting anything in return.

The First Row

·6·
Water in the head, fire in the eyes

YOUR STATE OF MIND

Superficially you seem animated with rather optimistic good intentions, for you feel immune to problems. But beware: in reality, your mind isn't sharp, your thoughts are confused or you have forgotten to think of the obstacles that could suddenly block your path.

IF YOUR QUESTION
   IS ABOUT ...
A specific project ~
Your chances of success are slim at present. You are blind to possible difficulties, you have a tendency to underestimate other people, or you entertain delusions. This figure indicates that others are unable to help you. They are themselves feeling confused or dependent, which prevents them from being lucid.

Water in the head, sand in the eyes

YOUR STATE OF MIND

This figure shows frustration, sadness, anguish or suffering. You are confused about what to do, where to go, to whom to talk. You feel dependent on someone or on a situation, and your vision is therefore blurred. Take care not to let your own anger, jealousy or resentment affect you too deeply.

IF YOUR QUESTION IS ABOUT ...

A specific project ~ Your chances of success are slim for you lack room to manoeuvre. At the moment, doors seem to be shut because other people – or another person – seem more determined than you are. Yet it would be useless to protest or fight. To make a new start, you need to set aside an idea, a desire, some aspects of this project, or to give without expecting anything in return.

The First Row

Water in the head, wind in the eyes

YOUR STATE OF MIND

On the surface, you seem motivated, joyful and satisfied with yourself. But the truth is that you feel upset and embarrassed. A particular problem keeps arising or you are angry or disappointed with someone. Your mind lacks clarity, and you don't feel up to making a new beginning or starting a new task. You still lack self-confidence.

IF YOUR QUESTION IS ABOUT ...

A specific project ~ You do not yet have very great chances of succeeding. People around you are themselves in a strange or difficult predicament and therefore are unable to understand what you seek. This is making you confused, or is causing your initial project to be re-evaluated. This figure indicates that it is not possible for you to get help.

 Wind in the head, fire in the eyes

YOUR STATE OF MIND
You are driven, enthusiastic and optimistic. Your thoughts are clear, your goals well defined, your dreams attainable. This positive attitude allows you to realize your desires. It is a very promising figure.

IF YOUR QUESTION IS ABOUT …
A specific project ~ Your chances of success are excellent. People trust you; they are ready to follow you and help you.

A journey ~ You will draw much gratification from it and you will return home richer, financially or spiritually.

The First Row

Wind in the head, sand in the eyes

YOUR STATE OF MIND

You fear failure or not being up to the task. You have suffered, have been hurt, or feel dragged down by a weight. These sad thoughts slow you down and limit you. Those around you are unable to help you, for their own minds are confused. If questions are piling up, if events don't seem to be working out right at the moment, you know in your heart that you are following the right path.

IF YOUR QUESTION IS ABOUT ...

A *specific project* ~ Your chances of success are good but they depend on your ability to seek reassurance. Positive influences will soon take over.

11
The three stars

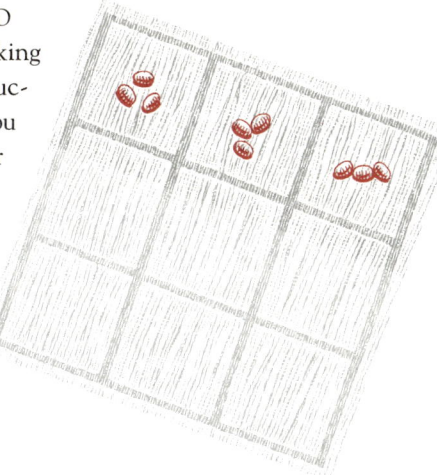

YOUR STATE OF MIND
You are capable of knocking down barriers and of succeeding brilliantly, for you are animated with inner strength, enthusiasm and mastery. You fear neither difficulties nor dependence from others. Your actions are guided and luck is truly your companion.

OMEN
These three stars protect you; you don't need to seek guidance through Kumalak. Things will turn out well for you – in fact, even better than you ever imagined.

The First Row

·12·
Wind in the head, water in the eyes

YOUR STATE OF MIND

Something is bothering you, you are angry with somebody, or you feel that obstacles are blocking your path. Nevertheless, you know deep down that you are following the right path, because this path reflects your deepest aspirations. But the people on whom you depend don't experience such clarity: they are so confused, in fact, that their very confusion influences you.

IF YOUR QUESTION IS ABOUT ...

A specific project ~
Your chances of success are good if you realize that your current problems are temporary; indeed they don't depend directly on you. Positive influences will take over soon.

The First Row

· 13 ·
Sand in the head, sand in the eyes

YOUR STATE OF MIND

Your mind is utterly tormented. You are assailed by questions without being able to find answers, or an obstacle seems insurmountable. You feel dragged down by a weight, you have lost your focus or you are afraid of being forced to sacrifice something. The people who could help you are distant, out of reach, or you can't trust them. You are very dependent on others.

IF YOUR QUESTION IS ABOUT …

A specific project ~ Your chances of success are minimal if you remain on the same path. You should set aside – perhaps for good – a desire, some thoughts or elements that are no longer realistic; or you should give without expecting anything in return.

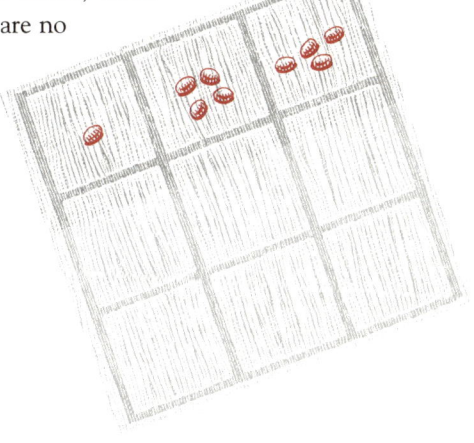

The First Row

14
Sand in the head, wind in the eyes

YOUR STATE OF MIND
You have everything you need to be happy except that you lack something or someone. You are torn apart, pushed and pulled in all directions. You feel the need to act, move, travel or try new experiences. However, you feel dragged down by a weight, your way forward is blocked, a past suffering is re-emerging, or a question is tormenting you.

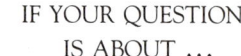

IF YOUR QUESTION IS ABOUT ...
A *specific project* ~ Your chances of success are not yet very great. You are ready to accomplish more, to do better to improve your situation, but those around you appear to be weak, indecisive and incapable of helping you. That makes you feel sullen.

15
Sand in the head, water in the eyes

YOUR STATE OF MIND
Your current situation makes you feel uneasy. You are unsure of what you are doing and what you really want. Your ideas don't match other people's, or those around you refuse to be influenced. You don't see how your dreams can be realized, and this makes you feel sullen.

IF YOUR QUESTION IS ABOUT …
A *specific project* ~ Your chances of succeeding are presently slim. You feel sad, disappointed and pessimistic. You lack motivation, and those around you are aware of this. You feel dependent, and you are finding it difficult to turn things around.

The First Row

· 16 ·
Sand in the head, fire in the eyes

YOUR STATE OF MIND

Your predicament is paradoxical. You seem strong and driven to progress. But deep down, you are tormented by a problem and you feel as if your desires can't materialize quickly. There is nobody on whom you can rely. Indeed, you are at a loss when it comes to figuring out what your loved ones expect from you. You may seem detached and confident, but you are hiding a fear of the future.

IF YOUR QUESTION IS ABOUT ...

A specific project ~ Your chances of success are not yet very great, for your mind is confused and you are unsure of the path to follow, as well as what choices to make. You are in tune neither with yourself nor with other people around you.

The Second Row

THE PRESENT

Heart

Intuition

Feelings

Impressions

Fears

Doubts

Struggles

Relationships

The Second Row

17

Fire in the heart, water in the hands

YOUR CURRENT SITUATION
You find yourself in rather a good situation for your heart is pure and enthusiastic, and your intuition tells you that you are following the right path.

YOUR STRENGTHS AND WEAKNESSES
You lack resources, calibre and conviction. The power struggle you are experiencing with your partner is tipped against you at the moment.

IF YOUR QUESTION IS ABOUT …

Love ~ Your partner seems to be demanding or selfish, and you long for a more fulfilling relationship. You are right to keep faith because your feelings are true.

Work ~ You are not in an advantageous position. You lack harmony in your relationships, or perhaps you lack financial backing or investment.

Health ~ You seem weak and anxious, but you have enough inner strength to get better. There is no need for you to worry.

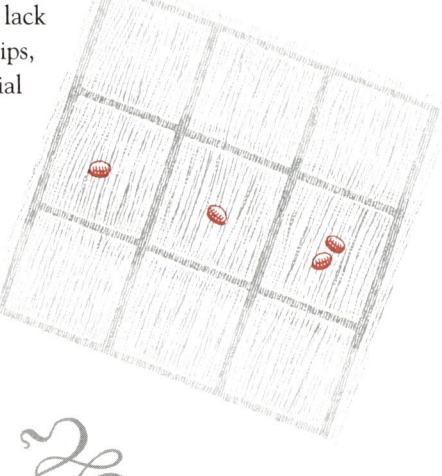

The Second Row

Fire in the heart, fire in the hands

YOUR CURRENT SITUATION
You are unable to take action or to take matters into your own hands for you are dependent on others. A job has been left undone, a relationship is unstable.

YOUR STRENGTHS AND WEAKNESSES
You are still lacking resources, strength or communication to improve the situation.

IF YOUR QUESTION IS ABOUT …

Love ~ Your partner's mind lacks clarity, but the ball is in his or her court. It isn't up to you to decide or propose.

Work ~ You are sincere, you believe in your project and that you are right, but you clash with people who don't seem to be playing the same game.

Health ~ You feel tired or very unmotivated, but you do have good inner resources. Don't rely on anybody as you will have to overcome your problems alone. Be patient.

The Second Row

Fire in the heart, earth in the hands

19

YOUR CURRENT SITUATION
You enjoy many qualities and your heart is full of good intentions. Those around you are willing to follow you, help you and trust you. One of your traits means that you are capable of great generosity.

YOUR STRENGTHS AND WEAKNESSES
You have the resources and spiritual strength to improve your situation, to engage in a new relationship or develop an existing one. Your intuition tells you that you are on the right path.

IF YOUR QUESTION IS ABOUT …

Love ~ You are a very passionate person. Your partner is ready to commit to you, to share his or her feelings with you. He or she values you, and this great relationship can only improve.

Work ~ You have the power to act and to decide. The figure shows financial improvement, an investment and an increase.

Health ~ Don't worry. This figure shows good health or fast recovery.

The Second Row

· 20 ·
Fire in the heart, wind in the hands

YOUR CURRENT SITUATION
Your current situation is rather good. You know what you want and you are ready to act on your confidence.

YOUR STRENGTHS AND WEAKNESSES
You have an inferiority complex with regard to others or you still lack self-confidence. Nevertheless, you are able to remedy these deficiencies.

IF YOUR QUESTION IS ABOUT …

Love ~ Your partner has many qualities and you are not mistaken about him or her. You believe in what you do and what you say.

Work ~ Your superiors, partners and colleagues are willing to help you. They are giving you the opportunity to improve and take on new responsibilities.

Health ~ This figure shows good health, renewed strength and recovery.

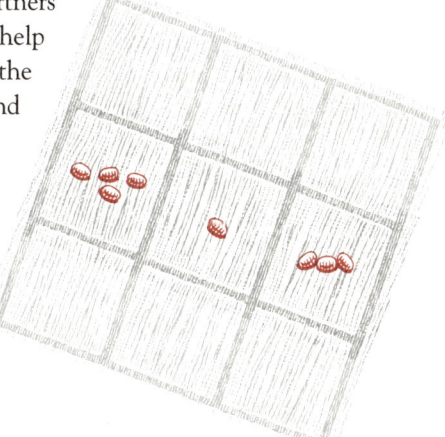

45

The Second Row

Water in the heart, fire in the hands

· 21 ·

YOUR CURRENT SITUATION
It is not to your advantage. Your heart is heavy and something is bothering you. Beware – if you don't change your state of mind the confusion will only deepen.

YOUR STRENGTHS AND WEAKNESSES
You lack strength, conviction and determination or clarity in your judgements.

IF YOUR QUESTION IS ABOUT …

Love ~ You feel torn apart and you no longer know what to think. The time has come to get to the core of the problem, to figure out what kind of life you want to lead.

Work ~ You do not hold the cards to improving the situation in the short term. You are totally dependent on those around you or you are being mistreated by the situation.

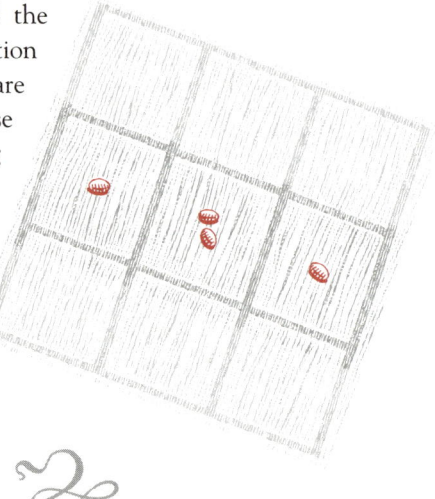

Health ~ Anxiety is a bad counsellor. If you continue, your health will be at risk.

The Second Row

22

Water in the heart, earth in the hands

YOUR CURRENT SITUATION
You don't really know where you're going or how you should behave. Your uncertainty is made all the worse because those around you feel the same way.

YOUR STRENGTHS AND WEAKNESSES
You possess strengths that cannot express themselves just at the moment.

IF YOUR QUESTION IS ABOUT ...
Love ~ You enjoy a wide range of feelings but your partner cannot follow you, and you take this very much to heart. The figure shows misunderstanding, embarrassment or a lack of frankness.

Work ~ You are capable of working hard and of making an effort, but your value is underestimated. This makes you sad and forces you to withdraw from this situation.

Health ~ Beware – this figure warns you about something worse. There is the risk of an accident, of a physical or mental illness. Don't hesitate to see a doctor.

The Second Row

· 23 ·
Water in the heart, wind in the hands

YOUR CURRENT SITUATION
You want to balance your relationships, to reach a state of harmony, but you feel nervous and tense. You are afraid of losing something and you are finding it difficult to see the situation clearly.

YOUR STRENGTHS AND WEAKNESSES
Your position is fragile for you lack self-confidence.

IF YOUR QUESTION IS ABOUT …
Love ~ Which of the two of you will have the last word? Certainly not you since your heart is not at peace. Regrets and fears prevent you from being yourself.

Work ~ You possess qualities and you want to express them, but those you depend upon don't share your vision. You fear not measuring up. Your will may weaken and doubts may overcome you.

Health ~ Don't fear anything. Your problems are temporary.

The Second Row

Water in the heart, water in the hands 24

YOUR CURRENT SITUATION
You are overcome by doubts. You are upset, tormented and worried, and this negativity is influencing your relationships. Those around you are using their power to crush you and then exploit you.

YOUR STRENGTHS AND WEAKNESSES
You don't currently possess the strengths needed to act or make decisions to improve your situation.

IF YOUR QUESTION IS ABOUT …

Love ~ You are unhappy. Your mind is confused, anxiety torments you, and you are unable to take action. Communication has broken down. You are engaged in a power struggle and you are losing.

Work ~ You are unable to gain a clear vision of your situation because of the doubts and fears that have overtaken you. Those you depend upon don't have the time or the will to help you soothe your tension.

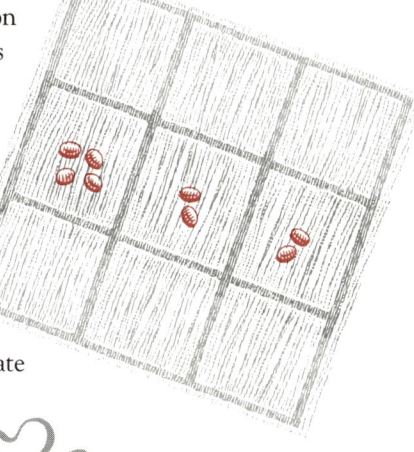

Health ~ There is risk of exhaustion, stress, illness or depression. Don't hesitate to see a doctor.

The Second Row

25.
Wind in the heart, earth in the hands

YOUR CURRENT SITUATION
Deep down you are joyful and receptive. You have all it takes to develop the situation in a positive way.

YOUR STRENGTHS AND WEAKNESSES
You enjoy great physical and mental strength. Your heart is open to the world and you are ready to try new experiences.

IF YOUR QUESTION IS ABOUT …

Love ~ You are in a strong position, capable of motivating, guiding and helping your partner. He or she is the one who lacks determination or enthusiasm.

Work ~ You know what you want, your plans are well defined and you believe in your success. Those you depend on cannot slow you down in any way.

Health ~ You have no reason to worry due to your strong physical and mental stamina.

·26· Wind in the heart, wind in the hands

YOUR CURRENT SITUATION
There is a great difference between your position and the position of others. You are motivated, confident that you will be capable of achieving your plans; you don't fear adversity.

YOUR STRENGTHS AND WEAKNESSES
You feel strong and capable of overcoming obstacles, but those around you don't enjoy the same luck. The scales are tipped in your favour.

IF YOUR QUESTION IS ABOUT ...
Love ~ The current problem doesn't come from you but from your partner who is anxious and tense: he or she feels dependent on you. Nevertheless, he or she is the one who needs to change, not you.

Work ~ You are capable of meeting challenges and making decisions, but don't rely on anybody to help you. Your boss, your partner or your colleagues are very confused and unable to contribute to your project.

Health ~ You have no reason to worry on this score.

A legal problem ~ You will win.

The Second Row

27
Wind in the heart, water in the hands

YOUR CURRENT SITUATION
You are dependent on others at the moment. This could conceivably make you sad, but in this case you are not upset because you are convinced that you are on the right path.

YOUR STRENGTHS AND WEAKNESSES
Your relationships are not working out well. You can neither influence them nor win the power struggle.

IF YOUR QUESTION IS ABOUT ...

Love ~ The balance and harmony you once experienced have gone for the moment. It will take a while to sort out this problem because your partner is determined and hard to influence.

Work ~ Those you depend upon are slowing you down and you don't feel capable of realizing your ideas anyway. Don't worry: this situation is temporary. The strengths you cannot yet express are without any doubt within you.

Health ~ You have no reason to worry about your health.

A legal problem ~ You are unable to fight because your opponent is more powerful than you.

The Second Row

28

Wind in the heart, fire in the hands

YOUR CURRENT SITUATION
You cannot visualize yourself as autonomous and capable of actions or decisions because you are almost entirely dependent on others at the moment. Nevertheless, your personality isn't affected by it, and you feel serene.

YOUR STRENGTHS AND WEAKNESSES
There is a great difference between your rather weak position and the rather strong one of others. At the moment you lack resources, qualities or arguments to improve the situation.

IF YOUR QUESTION IS ABOUT …
Love ~ The power struggle between the two of you is in your partner's favour. You do not yet hold the cards that will bring you a healthy relationship. You should lead instead of follow.

Work ~ Your projects are realistic and you are right to expect success. But you still lack the arguments necessary to convince your superiors, or perhaps your task is not yet at completion stage.

Health ~ The figure shows an illness, suffering or a weakness. This is only temporary, however.

A legal problem ~ You don't measure up to your opponents on this score.

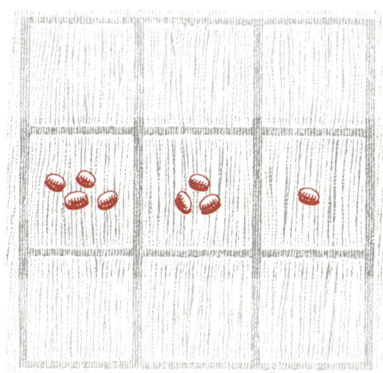

The Second Row

Sand in the heart, wind in the hands

YOUR CURRENT SITUATION

You seem disappointed and your heart is filled with sorrow. Your mind is flooded with questions, and you feel held up and stuck. However, this interpretation of the situation is not accurate.

YOUR STRENGTHS AND WEAKNESSES

You possess sufficient strength to carry out your project; this position allows you to use your assets, but you are overwhelmed by your emotions.

IF YOUR QUESTION IS ABOUT ...

Love ~ Your feelings are mixed and confused. You would like to express yourself freely, to clarify a situation, but your partner seems to be weak, stressed or too dependent on you. Even though he or she is willing to be guided, that is not what you need.

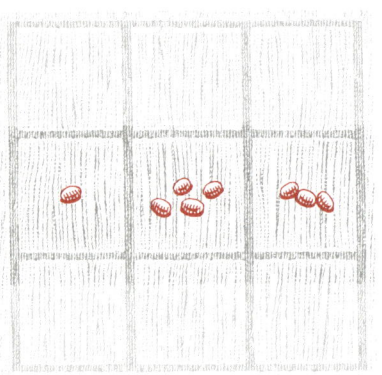

Work ~ You have self-doubts, and those you depend upon are incapable of helping you at the moment. They have their own problems to resolve, as well as their own weaknesses.

Health ~ You are worrying when you really shouldn't. If there is a sick person in your life, it isn't you.

Sand in the heart, water in the hands

30

YOUR CURRENT SITUATION
You are in a difficult, conflicting and very emotional situation. Your vision of things and people is confused because you feel sad, anxious, jealous or judgemental and you don't know who to turn to.

YOUR STRENGTHS AND WEAKNESSES
You seem lost and you are exhausting your strength by asking the same questions over and over again.

IF YOUR QUESTION IS ABOUT …

Love ~ Are you disappointed? Unmotivated? You seem to have difficulty shedding the weights, regrets and disappointments that fill your heart. Maybe you should rid your mind of a person or a feeling from the past.

Work ~ The atmosphere at work is not good. There is jealousy, unspoken feelings and judgements, or the goals you have set are not well defined. You fear being made to set aside an idea or a project.

Health ~ Be very careful, don't take unnecessary chances and don't hesitate to see a doctor.

The Second Row

Sand in the heart, fire in the hands

YOUR CURRENT SITUATION
Your thoughts are confusing, and you are full of fear, doubt or resignation. You are feeling tired and stressed, and this is preventing you from putting up a fight to resolve your problems.

YOUR STRENGTHS AND WEAKNESSES
You are not presently armed to overcome the obstacles in your way.

IF YOUR QUESTION IS ABOUT …
Love ~ Your partner is very independent, not very understanding, and has a great influence on you, which makes you in turn very dependent. To free yourself, there is one solution: to get away, at least temporarily.

Work ~ You have to face recalcitrant people who are not easy to influence and who make decisions on your behalf, slow down your progress and stifle your autonomy.

Health ~ This figure asks you not to take your health lightly. Don't hesitate to see a doctor.

Sand in the heart, earth in the hands

YOUR CURRENT SITUATION
This complex figure shows that you are rich in ideas, projects and desires. It appears that people trust you and are willing to follow you.

YOUR STRENGTHS AND WEAKNESSES
You are aware of this inner strength which longs to express itself. Why then are you so sad?

IF YOUR QUESTION IS ABOUT …

Love ~ You want to attain harmony with your partner, but have a nagging worry and feel that something unidentifiable is making your heart heavy. On the other hand, perhaps you know the reason deep down but are in denial.

Work ~ You possess great strengths, but someone may be jealous of you or may want to make decisions for you. This is confusing you and is making your enthusiasm wane. Your objectives need to be refined, simplified, and reduced to the essential.

Health ~ The problem you have is more mental than physical.

The Third Row

THE FUTURE

Obstacles

◆

Action

◆

Journeys

◆

Behaviour

The Third Row

Horseman of water on horse of fire

33

OMEN
You are guided by your impulses and passions, but you are not strong or stable enough to make things happen. For the time being, circumstances are bringing you to a standstill.

IF YOUR QUESTION IS ABOUT …

Love ~ You feel like casting off old habits and reinvigorating your feelings, but your partner is absent, too preoccupied with him- or herself, or unavailable. You will receive no help from that quarter.

Work ~ You need to take action, to show your qualities, and you would like things to speed up. But this is not possible at the moment, so you should try to be more patient.

A journey ~ You can't yet leave on your travels.

ATTITUDE TO ADOPT
Calm down, wait for better times to take action, and don't be frustrated if things don't develop at your pace.

The Third Row

34
Horseman of fire on horse of fire

OMEN

This figure shows action, mobility and movement. New experiences should be sought. It is a good time to travel, or move, and to transform or start a project. On the other hand, it is not a good idea to stabilize your current state.

IF YOUR QUESTION IS ABOUT …

Love ~ Your partner is tense and feeling stifled, which is preventing him or her from completely letting go and giving from the heart. You need to take control of yourself and act on your own behalf.

Work ~ This is not the time to reap the fruits of your labour or to assess what you have achieved so far. You have barely begun your project. Don't let your enthusiasm start to evaporate.

A journey ~ Be prepared for a journey.

ATTITUDE TO ADOPT

Be ready to start something, to uncover new horizons. Be hungry for freedom, independence and new discoveries. Don't stay at home or even in the same place. You will find the satisfaction you seek elsewhere, with other people or in an unexpected way.

Horseman of earth on horse of fire

OMEN
This is a very promising figure. The success of your project is close at hand, within your grasp even. This figure shows financial gain, success, meetings, well-being. You don't have to go anywhere because good news is coming to you.

IF YOUR QUESTION IS ABOUT …
Love ~ The figure shows meetings and news coming from a loved one. Someone is trying to meet you, and you will enjoy being together again. If you are a man, this figure shows a steady relationship, conjugal bliss or marriage.

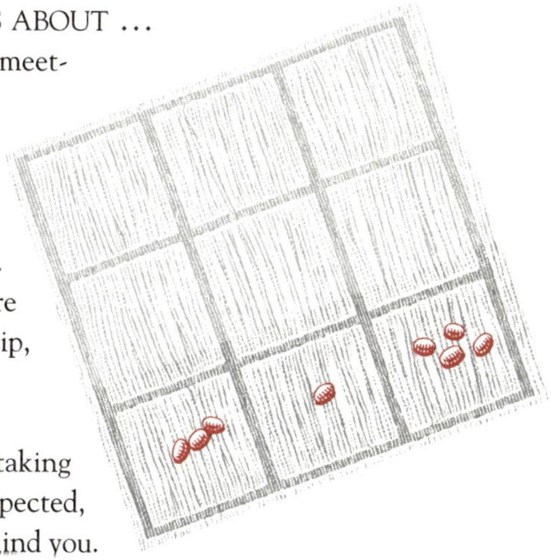

Work ~ Your projects are taking shape. Your ideas are respected, and people are rallying behind you. You are offered a job, and people are looking forward to working with you.

A journey ~ This is not the right moment to travel; be ready to receive good news instead.

ATTITUDE TO ADOPT
Be available and receptive because people are coming to you.

The Third Row

Horseman of wind on horse of fire

OMEN

This figure is very promising. The success of your project depends on your mobility. You are going to leave, to find what you've been seeking elsewhere. This is a promise of beneficial change and satisfaction.

IF YOUR QUESTION IS ABOUT ...

Love ~ Love is around the corner and it will happen, but you have to make the first move. Express your feelings, pay her or him a visit, or write to him or her. If you are a woman, this figure shows a steady relationship, conjugal bliss or marriage.

Work ~ You will gain great satisfaction from your project if you keep working at it. Find information, contacts and support.

A journey ~ It must happen and it will.

ATTITUDE TO ADOPT

Take a decision, act now. Get ahead of the situation by travelling, and you will be successful.

Horseman of fire on horse of water

OMEN
This figure is not very promising. It shows problems, disagreements, loneliness or a retreat you must make.

IF YOUR QUESTION IS ABOUT …
Love ~ Your partner isn't living up to your expectations, or a separation is about to happen. You must make it happen, change your state of mind, and look at the situation in a fresh light.

Work ~ There are tensions and misunderstandings with your boss, your partner and your colleagues. Reconsider your position, be capable of changing what must be changed.

A journey ~ There is an omen of danger, illness or complications. Be very careful.

ATTITUDE TO ADOPT
You are on the wrong path. Reconsider some aspects of your project that are not realistic.

The Third Row

Horseman of earth on horse of water

OMEN
This figure answers your question positively, but you must not be impatient, act too fast or expect support from outside.

IF YOUR QUESTION IS ABOUT ...
Love ~ The omen is rather good but you still need to clarify some aspects of your relationship and ease some strains in it, for your partner is unsure of his or her feelings or is not as open as you are.

Work ~ You will get some good news from someone in your immediate family or a more distant relative.

A journey ~ Success is within your reach but you have to complete the job you have started. Act with caution, don't offend anybody and rely only on yourself to carry your actions through.

ATTITUDE TO ADOPT
You are on the right path but some things still need to be resolved. You must persevere, do everything you can, and not rely on anybody to help you.

The Third Row

· 39 ·
Horseman of wind on horse of water

OMEN
This figure shows tensions and problems in your relationships. It reveals a power struggle, an opposition, a confrontation or a break-up.

IF YOUR QUESTION IS ABOUT …

Love ~ Tensions and misunderstandings remain between the two of you, and the situation is therefore idle. Each one of you fights for his or her own ideas and neither of you is willing to give up. You must come to an agreement, make concessions or become reconciled – say what needs to be said, do what needs to be done.

Work ~ You are battling in a confrontation with your superiors. If you don't make a move towards them, they won't approach you. Try to throw light on the situation before it becomes too confusing. Be ready to change direction.

A journey ~ It will happen, but obstacles are in the way.

ATTITUDE TO ADOPT
There is much antagonism between you and others.
You are going to have to find a new path as well as a new way of behaving. Don't wait to change direction, to change your state of mind or to make a decision, even if it appears difficult.

40
Horseman of water on horse of water

OMEN
Your situation will improve if you control your feelings. There are still inner tensions which you need to soothe as well as problems within yourself that need to be resolved.

IF YOUR QUESTION IS ABOUT ...

Love ~ The person you are thinking of will bring you harmony but you need to improve yourself in order for this to happen. If you are facing a problem, be aware that you are the one who created it.

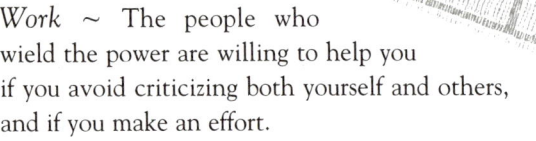

Work ~ The people who wield the power are willing to help you if you avoid criticizing both yourself and others, and if you make an effort.

A journey ~ You are not ready to leave on a journey in the near future.

ATTITUDE TO ADOPT
Learn to behave in a more straightforward and open way. Be more accessible, more receptive to new ideas. Then, and only then, will people come to you. Be aware that the final decision regarding your situation doesn't depend on you.

Horseman of earth on horse of wind

OMEN
This figure is very promising. Don't worry, the situation is going to improve a great deal.

IF YOUR QUESTION IS ABOUT …
Love ~ Your home is harmonious when it comes to your loved ones and especially to your partner. Your generous, honest and true feelings bring you closer. Yet you need to express them.

Work ~ This figure expresses satisfaction – success, financial gain and promotion. Nevertheless, to succeed you need to concentrate on the task ahead rather than travel or spread yourself too thinly among people or projects.

A journey ~ It isn't the right time for this. Stay where you are and luck will come to you.

ATTITUDE TO ADOPT
Be confident. You have all the qualities you need to live a better life. Don't seek happiness elsewhere: it is right in front of you.

The Third Row

42

Horseman of wind on horse of wind

OMEN
This figure evokes mobility and change. It indicates a change of mind rather than a material change.

IF YOUR QUESTION IS ABOUT …
Love ~ You want to go ahead and give a lot but your partner doesn't understand you. You need to become more independent. For single people, however, there is a promise of a romantic encounter.

Work ~ Be ready to travel, to adapt, to change your job or direction. Get away – mentally or physically – from the people you depend upon or from superiors who don't seem willing to cooperate.

A journey ~ It will certainly take place.

ATTITUDE TO ADOPT
Speed up the pace, don't let other people's lack of motivation influence you, and don't try to achieve more than you can.

The Third Row

Horseman of water on horse of wind
·43·

OMEN
Problems are about to be resolved, but there is an imbalance, a dependence. You are ready to progress but something or someone is in your way.

IF YOUR QUESTION IS ABOUT ...
Love ~ You are enthusiastic but your partner doesn't share your vision. The situation will improve only if your partner changes his or her mind and becomes more flexible and more conciliatory.

Work ~ The situation is still in deadlock and you don't have the necessary resources to advance your projects. You have to wait for the green light from your boss, colleague or partner.

A journey ~ You would like to leave but you cannot yet.

ATTITUDE TO ADOPT
The situation is not about to improve, but don't lose heart and try to rush things. The time has not come yet to act or realize your projects. Be patient.

The Third Row

Horseman of *fire* on horse of wind

OMEN
This figure brings a good omen. You must get ready to travel, or to seek elsewhere what you are missing here. Success will come from outside, and someone will help you.

IF YOUR QUESTION IS ABOUT …

Love ~ The person you are thinking of will bring you well-being. But you need to make the first move, to express your feelings, to go to him or her. For single people, this figure shows contacts, unexpected events and new relationships.

Work ~ Even though you feel somewhat isolated in your job, be aware that your superiors, partners or colleagues are ready to help you. It is among them that you will find answers to your questions.

A journey ~ A journey is likely to take place.

ATTITUDE TO ADOPT
Take action, communicate or travel. Exchange points of view because you are talking to the right people.

The Third Row

Horseman of wind on horse of earth

OMEN
This figure announces a very good omen for it promises the success of your projects, stabilization of your position and the fulfilment of your desires. Somebody is bringing you good news.

IF YOUR QUESTION IS ABOUT ...
Love ~ You are about to engage in a serious relationship, to deepen existing ones or renew your love life. Don't hesitate to anticipate the wishes of your partner: he or she seems to need you.

Work ~ The efforts you have made are going to be repaid in full. Your position is going to be strengthened and you will be offered a promotion or an improvement in your working conditions. This figure also shows financial gains.

A journey ~ A journey will contribute to your success.

ATTITUDE TO ADOPT
There is no improvement in sight at this time. Stay on the same path, without rushing. You will then receive good news.

The Third Row

46

Horseman of water on horse of earth

OMEN

This figure shows an isolation, a blockage, a lack of freedom. You need to wait for the tensions to dissipate and for your mind to relax before trying to influence the events.

IF YOUR QUESTION IS ABOUT …

Love ~ Loneliness, isolation, fear of failure … at the moment, you are unable to go towards your companion, and he or she cannot come towards you either.

Work ~ If the situation doesn't seem to be improving this is because you lack contacts, critical information or help. Don't try to force the issue, however.

A journey ~ At the moment, trips and journeys are not expected.

ATTITUDE TO ADOPT

You depend on others or you are trapped because of the circumstances in which you find yourself. You can neither get ahead nor be joined by someone. Don't try to act in a hurry, while you are angry or anxious. Be aware that this block is temporary. Those negative influences will soon vanish.

The Third Row

47.
Horseman of fire on horse of earth

OMEN
Your situation is going to improve a great deal. This figure shows wealth and well-being. You will soon receive good news from a much appreciated person who will contact you.

IF YOUR QUESTION IS ABOUT …

Love ~ Don't seek elsewhere what you have within your own grasp. Your partner is dynamic, and he or she will take the lead. Have faith in your companion to do this.

Work ~ This figure shows success, financial gain and a strengthening of your position. Your superiors or the people you depend upon are ready to join and help you.

A journey ~ This is without doubt a time to stay put.

ATTITUDE TO ADOPT
Success is here, before your eyes. There is no need to take action or to go on journeys; all you need do is to remain accessible.

The Third Row

·48·
Mother earth

OMEN

You have drawn the best Kumalak figure. It promises luck, success, good health, happiness and fulfilling journeys. Your dreams will be realized. You have talent, you are gifted, your thoughts are positive and generous. On a spiritual plane, you have wisdom, understanding and philosophy. When it comes to love, the figure shows harmony, understanding and shared love. Materially, it indicates wealth, acquisitions and expansion. You will reach your goal.

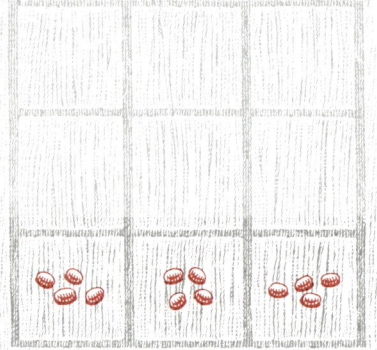

Reading Special Figures

After you have drawn your beans look at the grid carefully: it is possible to see special configurations. Look for them and understand them: they highlight some very positive aspects of your drawing.

Reading Special Figures

The Right-hand Column

THE RIGHT-HAND COLUMN CONTAINS ONLY ODD NUMBERS

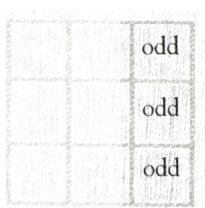

49 *Satisfaction*

This indicates good luck, expansion and a renewal of your situation. You will overcome all obstacles, and your wishes will be granted.

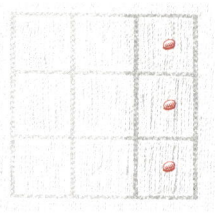

50 *Inspiration*

Thanks to your intuition and your sensibility, you have a very sharp perception of the situation. This figure means an omen of joy, happiness and luck, particularly on the spiritual level. You will make discoveries and fruitful finds.

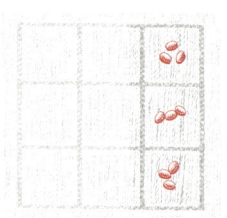

51 *Good fortune*

You have a gift for understanding others deeply and justly, and for feeling your surroundings. You have a very acute intuition and a very sound judgement. Your project will materialize. If you travel, even far away, you will be followed by luck.

Reading Special Figures

THE SUM OF THE RIGHT-HAND COLUMN EQUALS 7, 9 OR 12

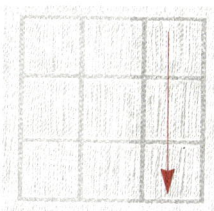

52 Chance

If the sum is 7 or 9 ~ You are lucky because this is a good omen. If you fight you will win; if you argue you will prove your point; if you travel you will profit by it.

If the sum is 12 ~ You will reach your goal, you will succeed.

Reading Special Figures

The Middle Column

THE MIDDLE COLUMN CONTAINS ONLY ODD NUMBERS

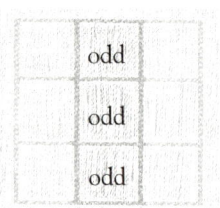

53 *Harmony*
You are at peace with yourself and therefore with your surroundings. Events will prove you right, you will be helped and you will succeed.

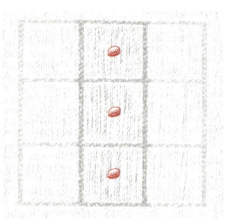

54 *The way forward*
This figure evokes a trip or journey. A path is at last opening up before you. It indicates a new direction, the desire to take off. You will soon be on your way.

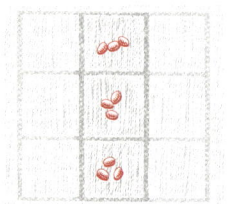

55 *Joy*
Excellent news is coming to you. You will be blessed with presents, happiness ... and joy!

Reading Special Figures

The Diagonals

Odd numbers in a diagonal symbolize news and bring some unexpected events in the near future.

THE DIAGONAL IS MADE OF ODD NUMBERS ONLY

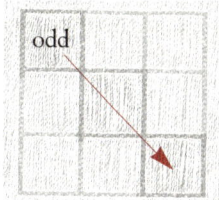 

56 News

You will receive news very soon, in the hours or days to come. It could be an encounter, a letter, a meeting, a visit or a phone call, for example.

THE SUM OF THE NUMBERS OF BOTH DIAGONALS IS EQUAL

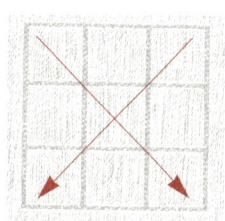

57 Balance

Your position with regard to the other person or people is well balanced. This figure is an omen of success in your ventures – especially if they involve a partnership or the signing of a contract. It also presages fruitful exchanges, harmonious relationships and happiness in your friendships or love life.

SAMPLE READINGS

On these pages are a few sample readings to show you how to read a drawing and how to make a coherent path from it. Pages 92–95 include record sheets so that you can keep a record of your readings (you might like to photocopy these pages so that you can use them more than once).

Sample Readings

1 · What is going to happen between myself and my partner? How should I act with him or her?

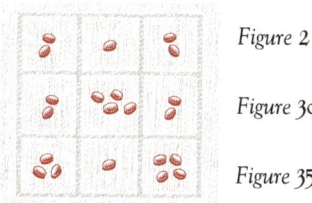

Figure 2

Figure 30

Figure 35

No special figures

2 FIRST ROW: PAST INFLUENCES

You have an acute need for affection; you want to get closer to your partner and find real harmony with him or her. You are right to believe that you can achieve this, and your chances of succeeding are great.

30 SECOND ROW: THE PRESENT

At the moment you are feeling anxious and lost, and you are wasting your inner strength with recurring questions. Your heart is filled with heavy thoughts and regrets.

35 THIRD ROW: THE FUTURE

Be reassured that the omen is excellent. It indicates happiness and that the one you love is coming to you. You will find harmony, and you will have plenty of reasons to be happy.

SUMMARY

At the moment you are sad and unfocused – perhaps even disappointed with your companion. You want to get closer to him or her, but you no longer know how to act, and this makes you unhappy. Be reassured that the situation will improve, and you will receive some good news. You will not have to go to your partner – he or she will come to you. Be receptive; happiness is within your reach.

Sample Readings

2 · I have been having some problems at work. What's going to happen, and what should I do?

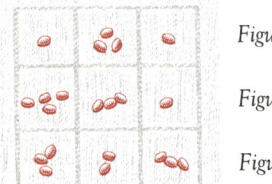

Figure 9

Figure 28

Figure 39

Special figures: 49, 56, 57

9 FIRST ROW: PAST INFLUENCES
You are driven – a winner – and your attitude is positive. This is an omen of success.

28 SECOND ROW: THE PRESENT
At the moment you are dependent on others. Either you don't yet have enough inner strength, or a job has been left unfinished.

39 THIRD ROW: THE FUTURE
This omen serves as a warning of a battle with people you depend on. You will have to make an important decision soon.

SPECIAL FIGURE 49 *(odd numbers in the right-hand column)*
This figure indicates expansion – a rejuvenation of your situation.

SPECIAL FIGURE 56 *(odd numbers in the diagonal)*
You will receive some news in the very near future. Be receptive to it.

SPECIAL FIGURE 57 *(sums equal in both diagonals)*
This is an omen of success. You are in a well-balanced situation with others around you.

SUMMARY
Your chances of succeeding appear to be good (figure 9). Nevertheless, your relationships with those you depend upon (such as your boss or your partner) are conflicting (figure 28) and will probably lead to a direct confrontation (figure 39). You need to make a clear-cut decision – even if this means moving in a different direction from those who are slowing you down. Don't delay: the special figures promise success.

Sample Readings

3 · Am I going to move soon?

Figure 15

Figure 27

Figure 40

No special figures

15 FIRST ROW: PAST INFLUENCES

You don't seem very confident at the moment, and don't really have faith in your project. Moreover, this figure makes no indication of a journey, therefore there appears to be no moving for you on the horizon.

27 SECOND ROW: THE PRESENT

You are dependent on someone to make a decision. Your companion doesn't seem to agree with your project. But this situation is not upsetting you deeply.

40 THIRD ROW: THE FUTURE

You are not yet ready to take a big step. You still have problems to resolve. The final decision doesn't depend on you.

SUMMARY

You will not be moving soon. Not only does moving not show in the three rows, but the right-hand column – the one that concerns you directly – doesn't predict any development. This row is made up only of twos, a number indicating difficulties. Fortunately, this predicament doesn't affect you deeply.

Special Readings

4 · Should I go on a journey that is being suggested to me?

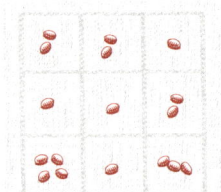

Figure 6

Figure 17

Figure 36

Special figure: 57

6 FIRST ROW: PAST INFLUENCES
You seem rather optimistic and full of good intentions, but you haven't given any thought to problems that could arise. Since you are asking about a journey, you should know there are some obstacles to overcome.

17 SECOND ROW: THE PRESENT
This project is making you anxious at the moment. Deep down, however, you have a feeling that you are going to leave.

36 THIRD ROW: THE FUTURE
This is a very good omen. This journey must take place, and it will.

SPECIAL FIGURE 57 *(sums equal in both diagonals)*
This brings an omen of success for your venture. Go ahead with it.

SUMMARY
If you are feeling anxious at the moment, understand that you will be going on this journey. It will bring you many benefits.

5 · No specific question

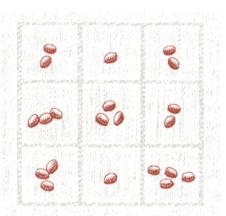

Figure 2

Figure 27

Figure 35

Special figure: 53

2 FIRST ROW: PAST INFLUENCES

You are seeking a partnership, a common cause, or you are trying to gather people around you. There is going to be sharing, meeting, help or reconciliation.

27 SECOND ROW: THE PRESENT

You will encounter some problems with another person or perhaps several people; relationships are not working out to your advantage at the moment. Nevertheless, you are serene and know you that are going in the right direction.

35 THIRD ROW: THE FUTURE

You are on the right path to achieving the connection or the sharing that you want. People will be coming to you. Encounters and unions are favourable.

SPECIAL FIGURE 53 *(odd numbers in the middle column)*

This figure indicates harmony. It also shows well-being, especially with regard to love.

SUMMARY

Your problem seems to be emotional since the two first lines indicate partnership and relationships. You would like to meet someone or to share your feelings (figure 2). At the moment you are feeling frustrated (figure 27) but the future holds excellent surprises for you (figures 35 and 53). You will be emotionally fulfilled.

Sample Readings

The Long-term Future

Kumalak may be consulted to gain a detailed overview of the future. To discover how a situation will develop in the long term, you need to consult Kumalak three times in a row. The first drawing indicates the short term, the second one the middle term, and the third one the long term. Very often, when taking three drawings, some figures appear over and over again. These indicate an important element of your situation and should be given most importance in your interpretation of the reading. The following two sample readings will help you understand how to make three drawings to gain insight into your own long-term future.

1 · Is my work project going to succeed?

FIRST DRAWING: THE NEAR FUTURE

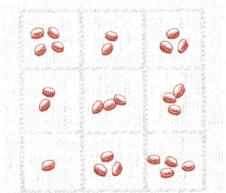

Figure 8

Figure 26

Figure 41

Special figure: 56

8 *First row* ~ You are driven but your thoughts are not yet clear.

26 *Second row* ~ You, and you only, are capable of making decisions, of bringing your project to completion.

41 *Third row* ~ Have no worries because the project which concerns you will have a successful conclusion.

Special figure 56 (*odd numbers in the diagonal*) ~ You will receive news related to this project.

Summary of the first drawing ~ You are driven and brave. Your project will almost certainly succeed in the short term.

SECOND DRAWING: THE MID-TERM FUTURE

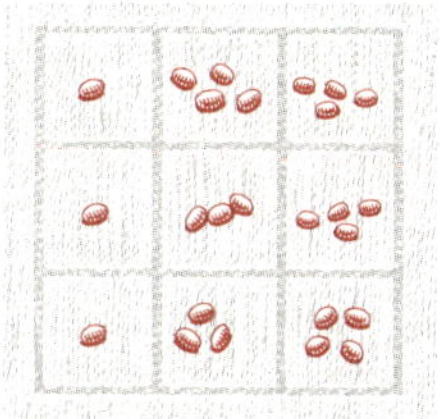

Figure 13

Figure 25

Figure 41

Special figures: 52, 57

13 *First row* ~ Your mind is tormented and you are afraid of having to sacrifice something. You depend on others to a considerable extent.

25 *Second row* ~ You enjoy good qualities, and the people you depend upon can't slow you down.

41 *Third row* ~ This figure reappears from the first drawing and emphasizes that success is certain.

Special figure 52 (sum of the right-hand column equals 12) ~ Your goal will be reached and you will achieve success.

Special figure 57 (sums equal in both diagonals) ~ This is an omen of success and of balance in your relationships.

Summary of the second drawing ~ In the medium term, good influences will keep flowing. You are on the right path. All the figures indicate success, except the first row (figure 13), but this is modulated by the second row.

Sample Readings

THIRD DRAWING: THE LONG-TERM FUTURE

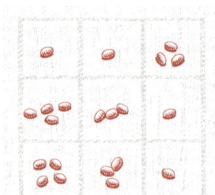

Figure 1

Figure 28

Figure 44

Special figures: 49, 53, 56

1 *First row* ~ You have drawn a very positive figure. Your chances of success are great.

28 *Second row* ~ You are almost completely dependent on others, but you are not deeply troubled by this state of affairs.

44 *Third row* ~ This presents a good omen if you are ready to take a trip or to seek help from outside sources.

Special figure 49 (odd numbers in the right-hand column) ~ This denotes that your wishes will be granted.

Special figure 53 (odd numbers in the middle column) ~ You will be helped to succeed.

Special figure 56 (odd numbers in the diagonal) ~ Good news is coming your way in the long term.

Summary of the third drawing ~ The fate of your project is brilliant in the long term.

FINAL SUMMARY

The three drawings can shed light on the initial question about whether the professional project will end up as a success. The drawings indicate that the project will succeed and, moreover, will not slide into failure in the long-term future.

Sample Readings

2 · Will our love endure?

FIRST DRAWING: THE NEAR FUTURE

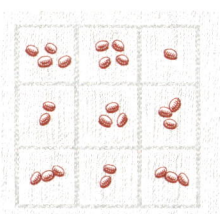

Figure 16

Figure 26

Figure 39

Special figures: 49, 52, 56

16 *First row* ~ Your situation is bothering you; a certain question torments you and you are afraid of the future.

26 *Second row* ~ Your partner is anxious and dependent on you.

39 *Third row* ~ There is a power struggle between you and your partner. It indicates that there is a conflict or a break-up in the air.

Special figure **49** *(odd numbers in the right-hand column)* ~ You should expect the chance to begin again, to achieve satisfaction by making a new beginning.

Special figure **52** *(sum of the right-hand column is 7)* ~ This is a good omen, and encourages you to act.

Special figure **56** *(odd numbers in the diagonal)* ~ You will soon receive some good news.

Summary of the first drawing ~ Your current situation isn't good. The three rows indicate anxiety, misunderstanding and a latent conflict. Your situation is changing. You must take action.

Sample Readings

SECOND DRAWING: THE MID-TERM FUTURE

Figure 3

Figure 24

Figure 34

No special figures

3 *First row* ~ Your self-confidence allows you to develop the situation and to motivate your partner to action.

24 *Second row* ~ You are troubled by doubts and worries; communication has broken down.

34 *Third row* ~ You are ready to try new experiences. Perhaps you will make an unexpected encounter.

Summary of the second drawing ~ Your situation is still developing. You are ready to try new experiences. There is insecurity and unfaithfulness in your relationship.

THIRD DRAWING: THE LONG-TERM FUTURE

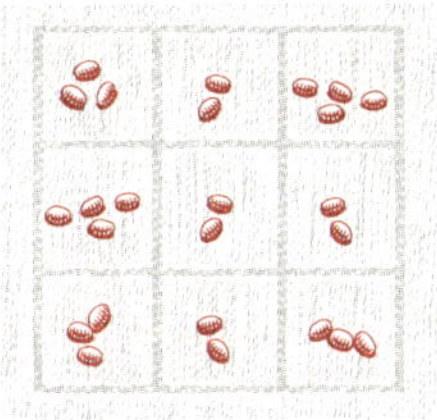

Figure 7

Figure 24

Figure 39

Special figure: 52

7 *First row* ~ You no longer know how to behave. You feel sadness, anger or jealousy.

24 *Second row* ~ This figure has reappeared from the second drawing. It confirms that communication has broken down.

39 *Third row* ~ This figure has recurred from the first drawing, and emphasizes that there is a break-up.

Special figure **52** *(sum of the right-hand column is 7)* ~ This is a good omen: if you fight, you will win. It is an encouragement for you to take action.

Summary of the third drawing ~ This drawing contains figures that appeared in the first and second drawings. The dialogue between the two of you can no longer take place, and there is an estrangement, a break-up.

FINAL SUMMARY

Your predicament is not good. Your relationship suffers from a misunderstanding between the two of you, and anger and jealousy compound the problem. You will need to renew your feelings. Your life could well be turned upside-down, but you won't turn back; you will not continue your relationship with the person you're presently with.

Record Sheets

DATE ....

☐ NO SPECIFIC QUESTION

☐ SPECIFIC QUESTION ....

....

....

→ First row figure number

→ Second row figure number

→ Third row figure number

Special figures

SUMMARY OF INTERPRETATION ....

....

....

....

Record Sheets

DATE ....

☐ NO SPECIFIC QUESTION

☐ SPECIFIC QUESTION ....

....

....

→ *First row figure number*

→ *Second row figure number*

→ *Third row figure number*

Special figures

SUMMARY OF INTERPRETATION ....

....

....

....

Record Sheets

DATE ....

☐ NO SPECIFIC QUESTION

☐ SPECIFIC QUESTION ....

....
....

→ *First row figure number*

→ *Second row figure number*

→ *Third row figure number*

Special figures

SUMMARY OF INTERPRETATION ....

....
....
....

Record Sheets

DATE ....

☐ NO SPECIFIC QUESTION

☐ SPECIFIC QUESTION ....

....

....

→ ☐ *First row figure number*

→ ☐ *Second row figure number*

→ ☐ *Third row figure number*

☐ ☐ ☐   *Special figures*

SUMMARY OF INTERPRETATION ....

....

....

....

Acknowledgements

EDDISON • SADD EDITIONS

Editorial Director   *Ian Jackson*
Senior Editor   *Tessa Monina*
Project Editor   *Kate Swainson*
Proofreader   *Michele Turney*

Art Director   *Elaine Partington*
Senior Art Editor   *Pritty Ramjee*
Illustrator   *Dave Hopkins*

Production   *Karyn Claridge and Charles James*

The photographs on pages 7 and 8–9 are reproduced by kind permission of Didier Blau. Original translation from French by Armelle Arriola.